The Patient Fox

by
Sascha Nieland Allard

George Ronald

George Ronald, Publisher
Oxford
www.grbooks.com

2025 by Sascha Nieland Allard

All Rights Reserved

A catalogue record for this book is available
from the British Library

ISBN: 978-0-85398-673-7

Illustrated by Dilmi Amarasinghe

Dedicated to the children of the world

The Patient Fox

While you wait for what you want,
you can play a game or sing a song.

Waiting's hard but soon you will see,
patience was worth it all along!

Felix the Fox
and his friends, Racoon and Skunk,
gazed up at a tree,
longing to climb up its trunk.

"I'll give it a try!" said Raccoon.
"Those green fruits look so yummy.
I can't wait to gobble them up,
to fill my empty tummy!"

"We need to wait longer"
Felix warned with great care.
"It will taste even sweeter
if we're patient, I swear!"

But Raccoon couldn't resist, and he quickly snatched a peach. Then he climbed even higher, grabbing more within reach.

With so much excitement,
he took a huge bite,
but it tasted so awful!
Felix had been right.

"It's hard, and it's stringy"
he sighed with a frown.
"I should have let it ripen"
he said, tossing it down.

Next was Skunk's turn -
"How about *that* tall tree?
It's bursting with pears
and there's enough for us three!"

Felix then said gently
"I wouldn't pick one of those.
They need more time to ripen -
that's just how it goes!"

"It's so bitter!" cried Skunk,
after taking a bite.
"I thought it would be softer!"
Felix, again, had been right.

Discouraged, Raccoon and Skunk
came down from their climb.
They stood by Felix's side
and agreed to wait longer next time.

Cheerfully, Felix said:
"don't worry, you two!
While we wait, I have ideas
of some fun things we can do.."

"We could play some tag,

or dance and spin.

"We could look for cool rocks to gather in our pail.

Or we could go for a hike and explore a new trail."

"And when it's *still* hard to wait,
take some deep breaths of air.
Soon there will be luscious fruits,
all around for us to share."

They waited many days,
and sometimes it felt draining.

But they continued to wait, without ever complaining.

At last, the fruits ripened - they were juicy and sweet. The friends gathered together to enjoy their tasty treat.

"I'm so glad we waited" said Raccoon with a smile. "I haven't had fruit this delicious in a *really* long while!"

"Me too," said Skunk. "It was truly worth the wait. We should avoid picking fruit too early – or late!"

With full, happy bellies,
the three friends agreed
that patience always bears
the best fruits indeed.

Discussion questions

1. What are some things you wait for every day that require patience?

2. How does it feel to wait for something you really want?

3. What can you do to make waiting easier?

4. How do you feel when you wait and then get something really special?

5. What can you do to help someone else feel happy while they wait?

6. Why do we need patience when learning something new?

Collect them all

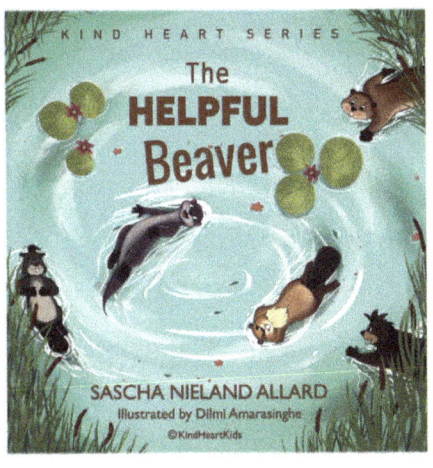 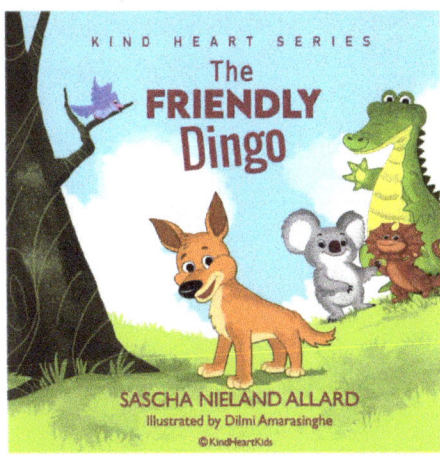 

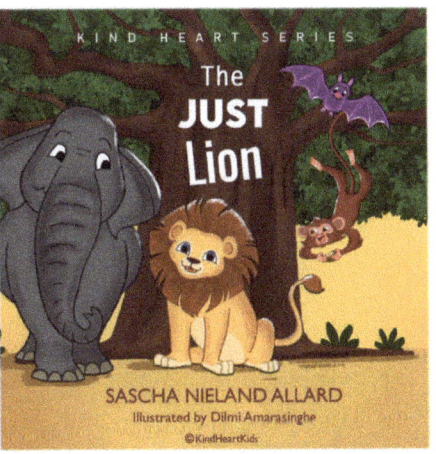 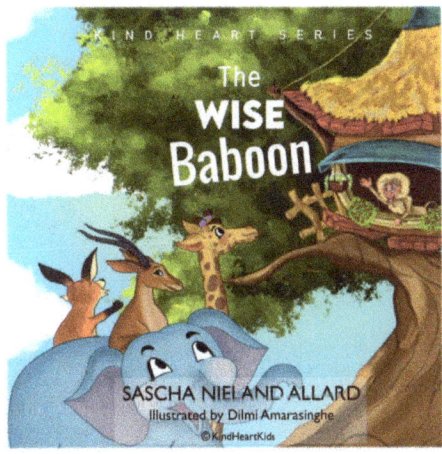 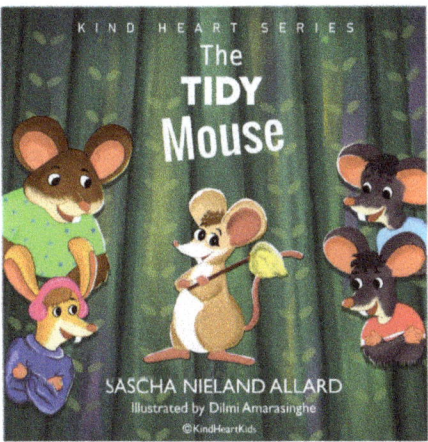

www.kindheartkids.ca
Instagram@Kindheart.kids

www.ingramcontent.com/pod-product-compliance
Lightning Source LLC
LaVergne TN
LVHW070949070426
835507LV00029B/3463